D1470132

Tunes for Trombone Technic

by
Paul Tanner
in collaboration with
Fred Weber

To The Teacher

One of the most effective and enjoyable ways to develop technical dexterity on an instrument is through melodies of a technical nature with scale and rhythm variation based on familiar melodies. TUNES FOR TECHNIC is designed with this in mind. Because tunes, melodies and technical variations are interesting and more enjoyable to practice, most students will work more effectively, and over-all results will be excellent. Some of the melodies and variations in TUNES FOR TECHNIC may be challenging and difficult. In this case work up slowly and accurately, then gradually increase tempo. In general, the book progresses in difficulty and correlates with the method book, "The Trombone Student," Part I, and may be also used in conjunction with any elementary trombone method.

The Belwin "STUDENT INSTRUMENTAL COURSE" - A course for individual and class instruction of LIKE instruments, at three levels, for all band instruments.

EACH BOOK IS COMPLETE IN ITSELF BUT ALL BOOKS ARE CORRELATED WITH EACH OTHER

METHOD
"The Trombone Student"
For individual
or
Brass class
instruction.

ALTHOUGH EACH BOOK CAN BE USED SEPARATELY, IDEALLY, ALL SUPPLEMENTARY BOOKS SHOULD BE USED AS COMPANION BOOKS WITH THE METHOD

STUDIES AND MELODIOUS ETUDES
Supplementary scales, warm-up and technical drills, musicianship studies and melody-like studies.

TUNES FOR TECHNIC
Technical type melodies, variations, and "famous passages" from musical literature — for the development of technical dexterity.

THE TROMBONE SOLOIST
Interesting and playable graded easy solo arrangements of famous and well-liked melodies. Also contains 2 Duets, and 1 Trio. Easy piano accompaniments.

DUETS FOR STUDENTS
Easy duet arrangements of familiar melodies for early ensemble experience.
Available for: Flute
$\qquad$ Bb Clarinet
$\qquad$ Alto Sax
$\qquad$ Bb Cornet
$\qquad$ Trombone

Contents

Old MacDonald

Pop Goes The Weasel

Yankee Doodle

Looby Lou

Sweet Rosie O'Grady

Nugent

Down In The Valley

Tramp-Tramp-Tramp

Geo. Root

Poet and Peasant
Waltz

V. Suppe

Sidewalks Of New York

Lawler - Blake

American Hymn

Keller

The Band Played On

Ward

Annie Rooney

Minnie Tee-Hee
The Indian Maid

Weber

There was once an In - dian Dame, Min - nie Tee - Hee was her name,

Her big sis - ter had more fame, She was Min - nie Ha! Ha!

The Victors

Ebel

Hungarian Dance Theme

Brahms

Theme From High School Cadets March

Sousa

Swanee River

8

Onward Christian Soldiers March

A. Sullivan

El Capitan Theme

Sousa

Rifle Regiment

Sousa

Home Sweet Home

Bishop

Joyce's 71st Regiment

Boyer

Entry Of The Gladiators March

Fucik

Theme From High School Cadet's March

Sousa

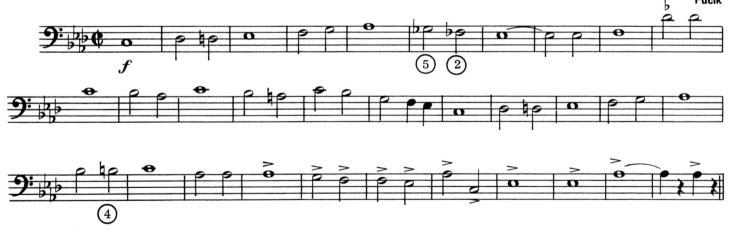

Sleeping Beauty

Tschaikowsky

S. I. B. A. March

Hall

Rainbow Theme

Chopin

Sakura Sakura
A Japanese Folk Tune

Rough Riders

Russian Melody

Long Long Ago

Long Long Ago

Birthday Greetings

In Key of F

In Key of E♭

Buffalo Gals

Up On The Housetop

Wearing Of The Green

The Erie Canal

Comin' Round The Mountain

Variations On A Famous Theme

Mozart

Melody

Rhythm Variation I in Key of E♭

Rhythm Variation II in Key of B♭

Scale Variation I in Key of E♭

Scale Variation II in Key of B♭

The Blue Bells Of Scotland

Loch Lomond

Our Director

Bigelow

Melody In F

Rubinstein

B.I.C.158

THEME AND VARIATIONS

The Dying Cowboy

Cara Nome

Verdi

Sharpshooters March

Metalo

Polly Wolly Doodle

Melody

Scale Fun

Marine's March

Melody

Fine

D. C. al Fine

Variation

D. C. take
Fine Ending

Can Can

Offenbach

Under The Double Eagle

J. F. Wagner

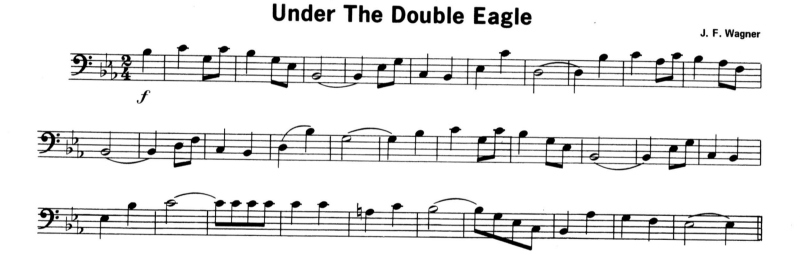

Father Of Victory

Ganne

Auld Lang Syne

Hymn Of Thanksgiving

Adeste Fidelis

VARIATION
America The Beautiful

Tonguing Fun
Moderato

Ward

Jewish Folk Song

The Violins Play

Paganini

Fine

D. S. al Fine

In The Gloaming

Our Team Will Shine

Ta-Ra-Ra-Boom-te-ay

Blow The Man Down

Tonguing Variation

Santa Lucia

Gypsy Rondo

Work out Carefully, then try for Speed.

A Technical Tune

Haydn

Fine

D. C. al Fine

Melody In Key Of C

A Tonguing Tune

Massa's In De Cold, Cold Ground

Andante

Foster

mf

ritard

The Eyes Of Texas

Melody By Borodin

Borodin

chaikowsky Concerto Theme

Tschaikowsky

Hinky Dinky Parlay-Vous

Merry Widow

Lehar

Song Of The Reaper

R. Schuman

Drink To Me Only

Gold And Silver

Lehar

Greensleeves

Moderato — 6 beats per measure

Carnival Of Venice With Variations

Theme From The Thunderer March

Sousa

Dance

Streabog

Fine

D. C. al Fine

Mail Call

Dance

Purcell

Mess Call

Use sixth position throughout.

Work out all Melodies on this page Carefully, then try for Speed with Accuracy.

Trepak

Tschaikowsky

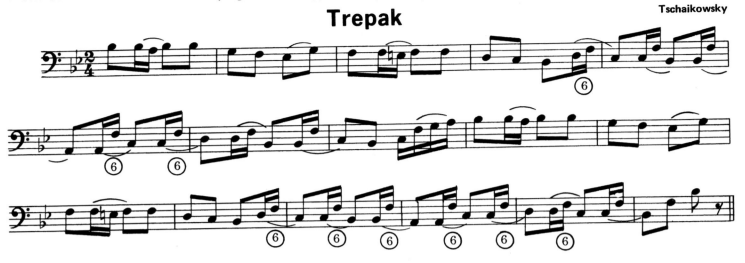

Variation On Yankee Doodle

Moment Musical

Schubert

Work out all Melodies on this page Carefully, then try for Speed with Accuracy.

Reuben Reuben

Technical Variation

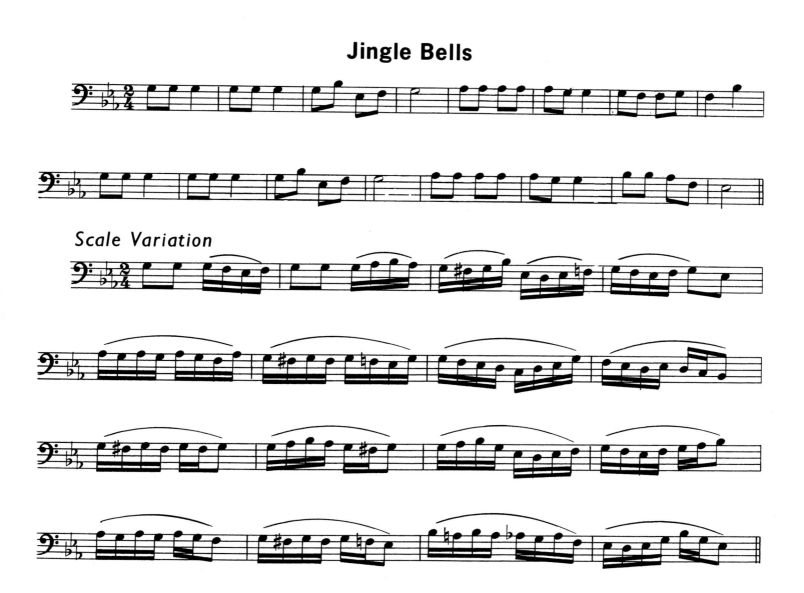

Jingle Bells

Scale Variation

Work out all Melodies on this Page Carefully, then try for speed with accuracy.

Morris Dance

Edw. German

Melody From The Opera Carmen

Bizet

Arkansas Traveler

Folk Tune